somelove

T0124892

some love

alex caldiero

Signature Books
Salt Lake City 2015

Design by Jason Francis

© 2015 Signature Books, a registered trademark of
Signature Books Publishing, LLC. All rights reserved.
Some Love was composed, printed, and bound in the
United States of America. www.signaturebooks.com

19   18   17   16   15   5   4   3   2   1

LIBRARY OF CONGRESS CATALOGING-IN-PUBLICATION DATA

Caldiero, Alex, 1949- author.
    Some love / by Alex Caldiero.
        pages cm
    "The poems in "Some Love" secretly yearn for rest but
plunge deeply into the scramble of human emotions. The
poems recall an emerging passion for performance, as well
as for the sensual liturgical marriage of physical space—the
church or temple proper—with bodily space."—Provided by
the publisher.
    ISBN 978-1-56085-243-8 (alk. paper)
    I. Title.
    PS3553.A394935S66 2015
    811'.54--dc23
                                    2015016242

for Setenay, some love

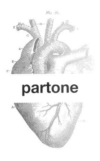

partone

"Your eyes are beautiful——they match."

—Bob Hope in *Road to Utopia*

Your hair
is a labyrinth
I can never hope
to get out of …

This is the beginning of a
love poem.

I'll just leave it at that.

1:07 a.m., 27 Dec 93

The changing face
of who would take
you from me
resembles my face

As long as it
was someone else's
it was easy
not to lose you

3:29 a.m., 23 Apr 94

Death found him working,
too beautiful to interrupt—almost.

Among the books
all covered with ashes
he looked for her image
in between the pages.

Dont bother
to become more beautiful.
Ignore the warning
that he might be lycanthropus.

In seeking gratification,
woman is no keener—man no blinder.

2 Aug 94

Between wishful thinking and clear perception
there is a gulf
that resembles the mouth of all the women
you will never kiss.

9:16 a.m., 29 Aug 94

My shoes know
how hard it is to be
without each other, so
why cant we learn that
contrary is okay? Left
right there,
it's what makes them
useful to each other and
to that other who
goes for a walk.

12:55 a.m., 23 Dec 1994

If (and only if) there is such a thing as
communication at a distance thru the
intervention of no medium save thought
itself by the mind fixed on its projection
toward its object by no rational or obvious
or known method other than the force that
impels or propels it as it were out across
and thru or translates it to the air, borne as
if on wind or wing to its destination by no
other means or conductor than the desire of
the projector who is both feeler and means
for it to spell the message of my heart to the
inner ear of she who is far both in thought
and place and by now out of mind except
for some chance recollection randomized
among life's various objects to take heed
and let enter as thought and yearning

3:11 a.m., 27 Apr 95

One day a hurt hits
with a fact and a sorrow.
It make me want not to
write. It make me want
to go away, to cry
in the arms of a lover,
past words said and actions
you cant take back not even in
a next life—on that day you
choose the one who
comes to undo you.

2:00 a.m., 4 July 96

Eyes
With nothing besides

Them there eyes
They look at me

Even after you're gone
I'm in their gaze

I close my eyes
Your eyes open

I
Stare as long as I want

Cant get your eyes
Out of my eyes

( ) yes
Let there be light

13/15 Dec 96

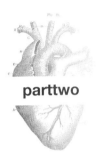

parttwo

"It's because an action has not been
completed that it is vile."

—Jean Genet

the flower
keeps me
from talking
about
the garden.

10:58 p.m., 2 June 93

an erection complicates the embrace.

11 Nov 93

I write my pain
and the words have no feeling.
I write my pain
and the words have no feeling.

1995

your hatred fits you
like a Mae West outfit.

a.m., 1 Apr 95

confessing my love is not unlike asking
forgiveness for a crime I didnt commit.

2 May 95

make your bed
now sleep on it.

make you beg
now weep for it.

brake your leg
now creep to it.

12 Sept 95

no matter how
much you hurt,
be specific.

21 Nov 95

cross between
bite and kiss—

days later
I still taste you.

13 June 96

for the nipple told me everything
I ever wanted to know.

7 Nov 96

(manage)

(ménage)

(mirage)

(marriage)

Nov 96

old fires

end in

meaningful

ashes.

12 July 97

How It Is

only eyes can account for what happens in
mirrors.

1997

her breasts discourage infantilism.

1997

Dreamt I kissed you
near your lip.

Woke up wanting
to eat ripe quince.

17 Oct 97

naked
skin
is just the beginning.

1997

take off
your armor
& be
amorous.

1997

you are so much on my mind
you have thoughts of your own there.

1997

Gift

once and forever long ago,
an ancient farmer gifted us
a bouquet of oregano.

1997

Her mouth on
my mouth—

in old age

I'll smile and
not know why.

2 Dec 97

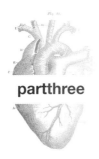

partthree

"Women are strangers in the country of man."

—Laura Riding Jackson

becoming less superstitious about relationships
makes the weather more predictable

a new freedom intervenes in the actions of the
body and the mind

body and mind are both one and two

body and mind are neither one nor two

black cat crossing the street

hat on the bed

the ladder, the mirror, the broken fingernail,

one cloud in the shape of a tree, another in
the shape of a snake

the unknown not getting any smaller

thinking the end is a new beginning

the final superstition mastered tho not cured

you find a companion for a part of you

what will the rest of you do? what if the
other also finds in you only a part and
has no use for the rest?

if you were to find someone in their
totality, how would you explain the
antipathy that might arise by chance
or just as part of the picture?

accept me as I am doesnt always work

change me into your ideal is no better

myriad forms of misogyny alienate you
from your own flesh

what are you doing in front of the mirror or with
your back to the mirror that reminds me of the
movies or of a wintry scene all white

you are taking down decorations from your body
as if a holiday of your life were over

what is it that gives your face an appearance that
makes me want to call you by another name and
meet you for the first time

the total effect is knowledge of every corner of
your mind as if nakedness were a way of intuiting
more inner places than your body can reach

astonished, we dont remember origins

29 Nov 96

unknown part of myself constantly out of
view, yet ever at my side, she walks, all that is
different and that I am not, my fear incarnate,
a warning from my mother about her own sex,
name I've called out in the night, closer than
my jugular, more intimate than autoeroticism,
knowledge betrayed, and as the ol' lady says,
women are strangers in the country of man,
and Solomon seeking after strange women
is clear, and the patriarchal injunction against
foreign women is obvious, the gypsy, a type
for that which calls a man to *woander*, Marlene
Dietrich giving Ray Milland a pair of golden
earrings, piercing his ears, the nature of
woman second to his, where second is primal
if not first, a vow taken in eternity to be the
other, or as the old crone says, a what-you-
may-call-it, a thing-a-ma-jig, a what's-her-face
or what's-her-name, oh ancient one, with a
sense of bitter delight in truth telling, with an
I-dont-know-what joyous verbiage, a cabalist's
dream in plain language, no uncertain terms

→

in no uncertain terms, terminating each word
with another all the way into the reader's
head, strings attached with no strings
attached, attachments and emotions thrust
out into the open daylight hues and midnight
glares of caspar-david-friedrich moonglow,
quiet eyes not quite closed, matriarchal, not
boastful prowess, not dormant, less strange,
even less so in the next millennium's together-
at-last romanticisms, end of uselessness that
doesnt contradictingly favor either——only
promiscuous hands would say more.

8:34 a.m., 3 Dec 96

partfour

"If you think we're together,
you're a poor judge of distance."

—Mae West in *Belle of the Nineties*

How careful
        should I be
with emotions that would unscramble
        every letter in my alphabet?

Perhaps then I could learn another language.

27 Apr 97

Flat as the paper
they're written on,
these words would slip
under your door.

Apr 97

We choose not to,
and there's heartache.
We choose to,
and there's heartache.

Not in the habit
of making known
what is closest
to the marrow,

feelings go where
possibilities
go when they are
impossible.

Apr 97

Under a face or under a stone—

The doctor recommends wine—

Drink and uncover.

Apr 97

The more this man burns, the weaker his sex drive. At first he couldnt understand, then he concluded that hidden forces were at work. He began to comprehend how devotees could go into fits and castrate themselves, how monks could keep vows of chastity beyond human endurance.

Apr 97

I bring my
hand up
and across
and caress
your face.

I've traversed
an ocean,
traveled from
one planet
to another.

All the while
beside you,
an impossible
arm's length
away.

2 May 97

Where nothing
can
take hold
words too
fall
nowhere near
you

May 97

Did I swallow it
in my sleep
as I opened
my mouth
to say your name?

Was it placed
in my chest
by some joker
to see me laugh
at my own pain?

Did it pass
from mouth to mouth
when you slipped me
the kiss that caught me
unaware?

O,
soften
this
aching
stone.

May 97

The fox is
a good omen.
But you dont
believe in omens.

The twin-tail
comet is a bad sign.
But you dont
believe in signs.

You pick up the penny
and give it to me.
You dont believe in luck,
but you know I do.

11 May 97

I break in no time.
But you bear words
as you bear seed,
taciturn, till
your body
betrays you.

May 97

A man's silence
and
a woman's silence
have
nothing in common

May 97

If
what lips say
contradicts
what lips do,
which are you
going to believe?

May 97

There's no one
from whom
to ask
permission

for words
that make
breathing less
mechanical

or feelings
that take us
into deeper
aching

May 97

partfive

"Forget about me, Kong;
can't you see, this is never gonna work."

—Jessica Lange in *King Kong* (1976)

This/That/Everything

If she calls within the hour
it means she will leave me.

If she comes to hear me
it means she still cares.

If she wears the black dress
it means she will make love with me.

If she strokes her hair
it means she has changed her mind.

I work out elaborate systems
of signs and significations

to explain her behaviors
toward me.

It's the only way I can
make sense of this relationship

to sustain me for those times
that it doesnt make sense.

I look for these signs
because at times they make sense.

22 June 97

Not
willing to open
or be opened
as if flowers
could refuse
to bloom or
touch so
intimate
a part
that apart
from it
they'd be
less themselves

a.m., 25 June 97

Round Trip

make 'm think
you want 'm
make 'm want
you real bad
make 'm feel
he has you
make 'm smell
you up close
make 'm touch
a little skin
make 'm see
you close up
make 'm say
what you want
make 'm move
over and over
make 'm ache
make 'm bleed
make 'm dream
about you
make 'm pine

→

make 'm long
make 'm sweat
around you
make 'm have
fantasies
hopes
expectations
then do
nothing
but have 'm
where you want 'm
where he willingly has had himself put
by every little thing you do that adds up to nothing
that promises everything including the moon
but delivers nothing but hurt so deep it dont hurt
so deep it dont seem like anything is happening
so down deep it dont feel like anything at all
until he's alone
then it all come up
then it all come out
it's only then
alone
that the truth o' the situation is evident
where there should be body
there's nobody
where there should be voice
there's a chasm

→

and a wall
so high
you cant see over
you cant stand on anything to see over it
so you stand on your own shoulders
in your mind
and see over the wall you cant see over
and see that it's over there
where you can never go
so you enter a capsule
in your mind
and go to where you can never go
and know for yourself you are not there
so you make a little room
in your mind
and step right into where you are not
and find you arent
but that's not all
in the middle of the floor
is a pool
you think how could such a little bit o' blood
do that
coming out of you a droplet at a time

→

unnoticeable

until you look down

is it coming out of your nose?

is it coming out of your side?

is it coming out of your ear?

is it coming out of you at all?

is it coming from some place you dont know?

so you take a step back

in your mind

a step back to the moment you met

and you're

face to face

eyes to eyes

you see what she sees

what she sees is not you

she dont know you

never saw you

from the beginning

you didnt exist

you never got out

of your selves

to begin with

this is where

it gets tricky

dont deny it

this is where

it gets murky

→

dont fight it
you didnt exist
for each other
so you went into
your mind
and made something
and what you made
made you you
made her who
you made her
in an instant
and now
in an instant
make h' think
you want her
make h' want
you so bad
make h' feel
she has you
make h' smell
you up close
make h' touch
a little skin

→

make h' see
you close up
make h' say
what you want
make h' move
over and over
make h' ache
make h' bleed
make h' dream
about you
make h' pine
make h' long
make h' sweat
around you
make h' have
fantasies
hopes
expectations—
then do
nothing

7 July 97

The way I love you has no mother and no sky
No door or rooms that I can enter
No food or drink no name or color no identifiable
    way to seek you out & find you
No wonder and no time to pass for its unfolding
A way for me to know what will never be
No roof & no floor, I'm surprised that I can
    remember anything about it
A long past event destined to appear in some
    obscure book on semi-mythical eras
The way I love you has nothing to do with you &
    me, it has no you & me, it is just a way to say
    how you & I would act in eternal stillness
A burning brand on the flesh for all to see
Plenty of space left over for what matters least,
    such as the contents of numerous drawers
    filled to the brim with so many little things
    begging to be written
The way I love you has no will of its own and no
    story to tell
No questions no answers and no sighs
No tears no movement no reason and no fear

→

No one to blame and no one to know better and
no one to forget and no one you wish you had
never met and no one who will lie or say what
you want to hear just to please you and no one
who has a name with the same initial as yours
& no one who writes home from a foreign land
and who will not return no matter who dies or
who gets married

The way I love you has no way out of its own
labyrinthine path from my house to the land
where people want to be loved but who are
not going to be

No ageless charm to commend my desire to
touch what is not here but which would appear
magically just for you

Caught up with the way you move toward me
as I recede into a distance never wished for
but nonetheless occurring because of the
movement of one of us in a direction we keep
secret even from those who have to know in
order to move us in that same direction

The only glass left full at a banquet for the blind

→

The way I love, you must be able to empty me
    and reverse me capsize me hang me upside
    down undo me and position me like a cup
    covered by its own saucer
To leave me alone so totally that I cant see my
    own shadow and call myself by name and
    realize how it feels to be the knock at the
    door and the ear that hears it and the mind
    that thinks it should open it but never does
    because there's no one there to open it but the
    very person who is knocking
To leave me clean under a clear sky next to a
    young cherry tree beside a stone to the side of
    the path on the way back to the house where I
    was born
To leave me breathless before my own
    cantankerous laughter with no time for
    counting no time for telling no time for the
    ever growing restlessness back to your arms
    unsaying what needs to be said over & over
    until I can remember without cue or clue the
    way I love you—

5 Aug 97

She says she likes
the exquisite pain of poetry
and that she isnt
going to respond or change
her mind and he must get
over this somehow and poetry
promises relief, but
it just fans the fire
& it's a con-
flagration of words and feelings
she enjoys because
it's cold out there in
reality, predictable,
the separateness in everyone's
life,
but it's good to feel
an impact,
to hear
desperate words &
imagine what could
but mustnt be—
it's more delightful
to see a poet martyred
than a saint:
poets cry out
in delicious agony,
while saints waste away
in proud silence.

13 Aug 97

Fire knows your name.

Says she's got something on her mind.

Dont tell, dont tell.

Because there are two candles
         dont mean there are
                    two flames.

The mirror tells the same old lie.

Dont stop, dont stop.

Light
          ends in
                       invisibility.

8 Sept 97

She dont notice
the sand

Leaking out of
her mouth

Her lips moving less
& less

They freeze into
a grimace

One eye
wide open

The other
blinking fast

25 Sept 97

Dont make a martyr of your
self for the sake of having people
stop and stare at your stigmata.

Even tho it's only paint, they
come up real close to poke
their fingers in the wounds.

7 Oct 97

Table for Two with One Chair

The room is in the middle
as far up as down,
as far left as right.

You played there as a child
only to leave
when you recognized the door.

The room disappears
from under your feet,
yet there is no falling.

You're dreaming the
words you're telling me
without knowing what language.

It'd be helpful
if you would return
my heart to my body.

Oct 97

I couldnt laugh any more.
My mouth became a
sore, words were cancerous
growths on my skull, and you were
my shadow who never could
move in sync with my body. I
couldnt sing "me and my shadow"
without feeling betrayed
and made to look foolish
in the semi-darkness alone
thinking that maybe I wasnt.
I'd make signs and gestures
to simulate scary creatures
so I'd be less afraid of the night.

22 Oct 97

Song

Make sure the eyes
dont meet.
Keep your thoughts to
yourself.
Numbers and words
line up.
It's just as well
you dont.

Nothing but eyes
closed tight.
You are the one
to freeze.
Cut off alone
and still.
You'll never know
what hit.

→

There now you see,
dont you?
See it còmìng
for you.
What ìt ìs ìs
not clear.
What it does is
not known.
But it's òrìgìn
is you.

From you to you
and back.
Dont say cant be,
it is.
Dont try to leave,
you cant.
Tongue-tied,
dont look into
her eyes.

23 Oct 97

So we found out how babies
were really made and what
really went on behind
closed doors or on the
other side of the dark
screen. We finally under-
stood what it took for a
cloud to be formed & what
the lightning bolt
actually looked like,
the shape of the earth and
the size of the sun in a red
portion of our world.
You could say
that the world is so big
& we so small,
that if we fall asleep
its perfume could suffocate
our heavy meat mind.

28 Oct 97

For instance ,
I'm afraid to be so
intimate with you that I
would discover you were afraid
of intimacy . So , keeping a
distance brings us closer , in the
long run , than if we were to be-
come mystically one , or
by some chance , run
into each other's double
and set up house without
any questions or suspicions ,
each of them and each of us
talking and eating and walking
without the slightest clue or
awareness . And it's all right
like this , because who ever
said life had to be lived by
our selves alone ? —It's not un-
usual to want to sing at this
point .

28 Oct 97

Words know they can enter thru the eyes or ears and be near you in ways I can never hope to be. They can stand naked in front of you as natural as flowers. Words can touch you with hands you'd never turn away, and kiss your mouth as you read them aloud to yourself. The freedom they enjoy with you I cant imagine. Words want nothing to do with me when it comes to you. They know I cant bare to think them so close to your most intimate thoughts. They insisted that I send you this, and I have.

4 Nov 97

She plays
a toy piano
She sings
a toy song
She thinks
toy thoughts
And when
it rains,
tiny toy
drops seep
into her
toy soul.
She knows
this is so
and wants
it so
and so
it is.

12 Nov 97

Because the telephone makes your voice so
small, I dont want to call you up. Such diminution
is unbearable when everything else about you is
already disappearing. I yearn for a close-up—to
see the salt on your skin.

18 Nov 97

In the goofy morning light
     a hand holds itself

Last night in moist sleep
     tongues came home to roost

Mouth language understood too
     quickly and forgot

Flavors of past wines
     another kiss come home

Before silence's open door
     chastity keeps still

Hands begin to do
     what bodies dare not

4:30 a.m., 22 Nov 97

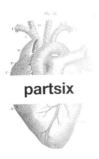

partsix

"You're easy to dance with."

—Fred Astaire in *Holliday Inn*

Encryption

with no slip-ups and in perfect control over
manifestations to others of any trace of inner
happenings, taking into account every smell
of contact, nothing that would betray any
touch, feeling, or thought that might point to
and implicate one or the other, disassociation,
without exception, struggling to be in every
way completely in harmony, committing no
mistake and having no reaction that would
tally up unknown quantities with unknowable
qualities, nor lead by any manner of inference
to detection of any kind of relationship or
connection, without any contradiction or mental
reservation, nothing, not then, not now, not
ever, nonexistent from the beginning, not by
nature, accomplished against nature, with no
smile no frown no body-language, no this-
that-if-or-but about it to cause the slightest
suspicion that would give away this emotion

1:30 a.m., 16 Apr 98

You never kissed
me. I never wrote
you poems. You
never told me how you felt.
I never did anything
about it. We never knew each
other's secret longing—

shadows
vanish
underfoot

12:30 a.m., 24 Apr 98

She asked me
with my mouth
"Do you think
about me?"
"Yes" I said,
also with my
mouth, "I
think about you
almost every day.
And you?" I
said wanting to
really know
but without
moving my lips.
"Yes" she said,
also without
moving my lips,
"I think of you
often and wish
I could say more,
but dare not.
You dont know
how I get." Then
→

she added:
"Forgive
me if I dont
respond." She
said this using
my mouth, and
with my mouth
I said, "I'm
trying to under-
stand why this
must be so." I
stopped moving
my lips.
I could feel
the tooth that
had been worked
on. I could
feel the tongue
searching for the
taste it swore
it wouldnt
ever forget. It
finally found it
in the middle
of my bottom lip. still
there. impossible
taste. tasted

→

with tongue tip,
and with tongue
I could speak it back
to her moving her
lips mouthing
the words with her
voice as she dreams
what I'm saying
speaking it out loud
in the morning
remembering and
saying it again
with her mouth
with my tongue
with her voice
with my words
with out questioning
moving our mouths
together co-
incidentally
words in both
of us say equally
you she me then
→

when us make
sure hear each
other clear some
water cross
over some
too long now
for not who
boon too far
my on for rain …
I found your name
hidden in texts of
my own making long
before we ever met,
your name and also
directions to your
house of cards
I dare not approach,
to your gossamer
hair I undo
with my breath,
not moving
my mouth.

ca. 2 a.m., 14 May 98

In Tongues

When my tongue
meets your tongue
it wants to play tag,
it wants to play hide-and-seek.

Then fatigued,
it would lie down
in its own moist bed
alone to dream in flavors.

14/15 May 98

then (this one word tips the discussion in an entirely new direction and realigns occurrences and works out conclusions like nothing you'd expect and that's okay because you want to change the course of your life, you want to accept the consequences implied in the aforesaid change and freely embrace another world and another way with no *what if I had done it what would have happened and where would I be now?* (complete acceptance of the fact without which life would be meaningless, namely that he wasnt going to change anything or any one, that it would not have any impact on his views and that neither he nor she would be any wiser for the experience. The other facts were just as important but not worth mentioning because of that very fact, that is, that it wouldnt make any difference. Yet it was clear: he would act the parts, she would act the parts, and together the drama would take logical & random turns as events worked themselves out (not necessarily for the betterment of either))) their story could be told without being spelled out beforehand.

1:20 a.m., 22 Jan 99

it is after, but we must understand what this means, way before it is after. it is also strange. it is worth investigating and perhaps finding out what came to me just in time to disappear as I stood talking with you exactly where I am right now, no less communicative than I'll be after I'm gone, once and for all, all at once, once at the point of no return (as is every point, even the redundant). so you are after, too late curious, my hand navigating your hair, then down, that is, over, opening what wet warm wonder

17 Aug 99

Stanzas (Rooms)

at cards
or love,
I lose at
both so
I stay home
for dinner

.

as we sleep
blankets stir,
by morning
a makeshift
wall divides
our bed in two

.

window
open,
it rained all nite
the floor so wet
we could
slip

→

•
sleep-caked eyes
cannot open
all the way,
it hurts to look
tho
wide awake

•
abruptly
a
rope
snaps, a
tightness
lingers

29 Sept 99

Orphic

that words could
                    clothe
as flesh would
                    enliven
as blood could
                    these bones
that he would
                    call back to life.

23 Nov 99

Admit
That we are together by chance
That another combination is as possible
That there is no one-and-only
That we will be caught with our hearts laid bare

We is not a word for us and us not a word for
both and both not a word for two and two not a
word for the number of those who would count
themselves together in the same breath and
thought or stand next to each other on the same
ground one-on-one or one-to-one or one-another
or another-one

Admit
We are together by chance
Another combination is as possible
There is no one-and-only
We will be caught with our hearts laid bare

15 Feb 00

Putty in your hands
Don't say I'm hallucinating
You look like a million bucks
You go out dressed to kill
How can I help thinking
What I'm thinking
What man wouldnt make a fool of himself
Oh my love, forgive me for
Wanting you all to my self
I understand and it's alright
Whatever you do putty in your hands
And dont say how can I help thinking
You look like a million bucks
You go out dressed to kill
What I'm thinking
Putty oh my love
I understand and dont say I'm
Hallucinating what man wouldnt
Say I'm hallucinating
You go out like a million bucks
To kill thinking
What man in your hands

→

Oh my love forgive wanting you
I understand to my self
Putty in you thinking
Wanting you dressed to kill
In your hallucinating look
Dressed thinking what man
Fool my love you understand
Whatever how you look
Dressed thinking putty
Understand hallucinating
Say a million bucks
In your hands
Wouldnt love understand
In you wanting hallucinating
Thinking understand
How putty understand
A million hands
Fool—

4 a.m., 19 Mar 00

flesh reminds me of wounds, wounded flesh reminds me of you, you wound my flesh and it reminds me of this nearby, slowly widening circle of blood which reminds me to gather dead branches and take out the garbage on this early spring day when I would walk and laugh if it were not for my crippled foot which reminds me not to sleep too much so I wake up feeling nauseous and so ill at ease my breath doesnt want to return but makes it back nonetheless, after all it is up hill and fairy tale characters are waiting to sing, and not knowing the words makes their songs more mysterious, which reminds me not to mistake tears for eyes, clothes for flesh, flesh for wounds, which reminds me

5:15 p.m., 27 Apr 00

Her awareness is the product of an overripe
attention to sense data fixed on the outer
because every inner thing is coated black.

Her senses probe overwhelmingly detailed
information so bent outward that looking
back would turn her to salt.

25 June 00

There is no body in that room waiting for you.
That room is empty and that bed is cold and
that light is the same light you left on. You
were there alone and so you left and went out
for a drive to reorient yourself and to search
for the wisdom to accept the fact that you are
alone and that there is no one waiting up for
you in that room and the light you see coming
from under the door is the very same light you
left on and you want to think and feel for a
moment that maybe you are wrong and there
is someone waiting there that she is there
waiting but you got to say it before you enter
you got to say it and say it with full conviction
to lessen the blow and the disappointment
you got to stop right there before you open
the door and say that there is no body in that
room and that bed is cold and that's how it
is say this without any doubt or mental or
emotional reservation just before you open the
door that there is no body waiting there and
so it is that the door opens and your eyes go

→

right to that spot and you were right you were
not dreaming you were not fooling yourself
not at all for indeed there is no body in the
room and the bed is cold and the light is the
light you turned and left on when you went for
a little drive to orient yourself and search for
the wisdom to accept the fact that is staring
you right now right in your face that the room
is empty and the light is the light you left on
which you now turn off and the darkness
rushes in and fills the room and you hope that
you do not drown

2 a.m., 5 Aug 00

Falling apart we cast off what isnt us.
Can we learn to hold on to nothing?

The way this works is called miraculous.
With that said can we figure out the rest?

Stops and moves make a difference in our life.
Does wishing give us more than a chance?

Drawn conclusions help us figure out the signs.
Ungrounded, shouldnt we resemble two wings?

A good rule is: dont finish until the end.
What alphabet must we learn to truly speak?

Feb 01

Poi c'è il sospiro
che assomiglia un fiato
come un vento
assomiglia una mano
che solleva la pagina
d'un libro muto.

Then there's the sigh
that resembles a breath
the way a wind
resembles a hand
that turns the page
of a mute book.

19 Feb 02

Lovers keep telling and retelling their stories. It's an automatic spectacle that continues to bring up flotsam till swimming is no longer an option. A thousand words a minute twenty hours a day for the rest of our lives would not be enuf. — stop punto. punto e contrapunto. senza virgola. punto e fine e via di seguito. senza dubbio without a doubt. ecco la causa della luce della voce della veloce della velocità of love.

30 Sept/Oct 03

partseven

One year from later

It's not gonna matter

That he got hurt

That she was unfair

That falling down

Seemed a good idea

Jan 00

We put it in a sack.
Drove out to the open sea.
Took a boat ten miles out.
Dropped the sack into the icy water.
This morning, there it is at the door.
We are more than horrified.

27 Jan 00

What life would distort
Practice would perfect
And what seems to die
Knowledge would restore
And time release us
From blame or blaming

4:30 a.m., 24 Mar 00

Unless you mistake
what you say for what you think
and find the answer
before the question
when your words begin to sing,
you make sense only when you laff

25 Mar 00

Words want so much to speak
to you, they come together
as this mind and approach
you as one does another
who may seem rude but is
just full of anxieties

27 Mar 00

My being

Human props

Up my absence

Against my presence

Leaves me standing

Outside both

30 Mar 00

Twenty-five years
to learn to speak,
another twenty-five
to know what to say,
twenty-five more
to say it

30 Mar 00

When Cupid lashes out—
Dont try to protect yourself—
Bear the whipping—
No way you can come out unscathed—
Bite down hard—
When Cupid lashes out—

10 Apr 00

Because I was so sure
of the meaning of the word,
I didnt look it up,
but maybe I should have
because the one I heard
was not the one she spoke.

10 Apr 00

Communication is complex
multi-layered and at times
labyrinthine and it's not
unusual to lose your way
when she thickens the plot
with a quick wet kiss.

3 May 00

to sleep not
wanting to sleep not
wanting to turn out
the light not wanting to
read the mind's
black scrawls

13 May 00

thing is: deny
it.
straight faced: say
you dont see it.
blush
if anyone asks.

16 May 00

the five senses all say the same thing
five senses all see the same thing
senses all taste the same thing
all hear the same thing
smell the same thing
I clear my throat before singing

20 May 00

my refrain

yr avalanche

my clear day

yr departure

my debacle

yr sleeplessness

26 May 00

As if in death
there could be
answers,
you utter your bleak thoughts,
fearless of the black fixtures
that you set up in your soul.

2 June 00

Dont be a mind reader.
Take and accept
what comes your way
with naturalness,
humility, and yes, grace—
You are part of the food chain.

23 June 00

Nonchalantly
                I open my
side, take out my heart, hold it,
still beating, in my hands, & insist that
everyone come close & verify that
this is no trick.

26 July 01